This Book Belongs To:

COLOR TEST PAGE

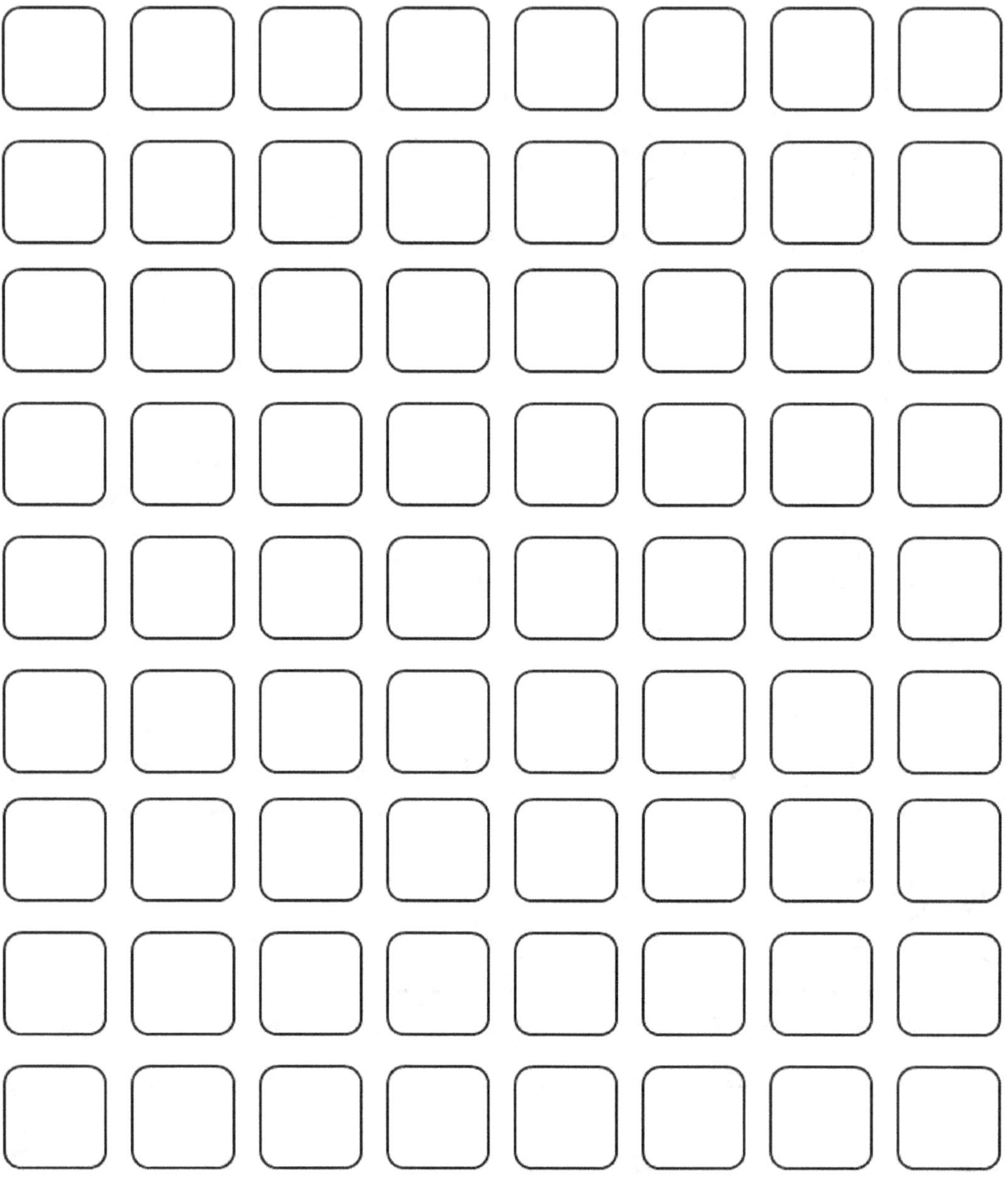

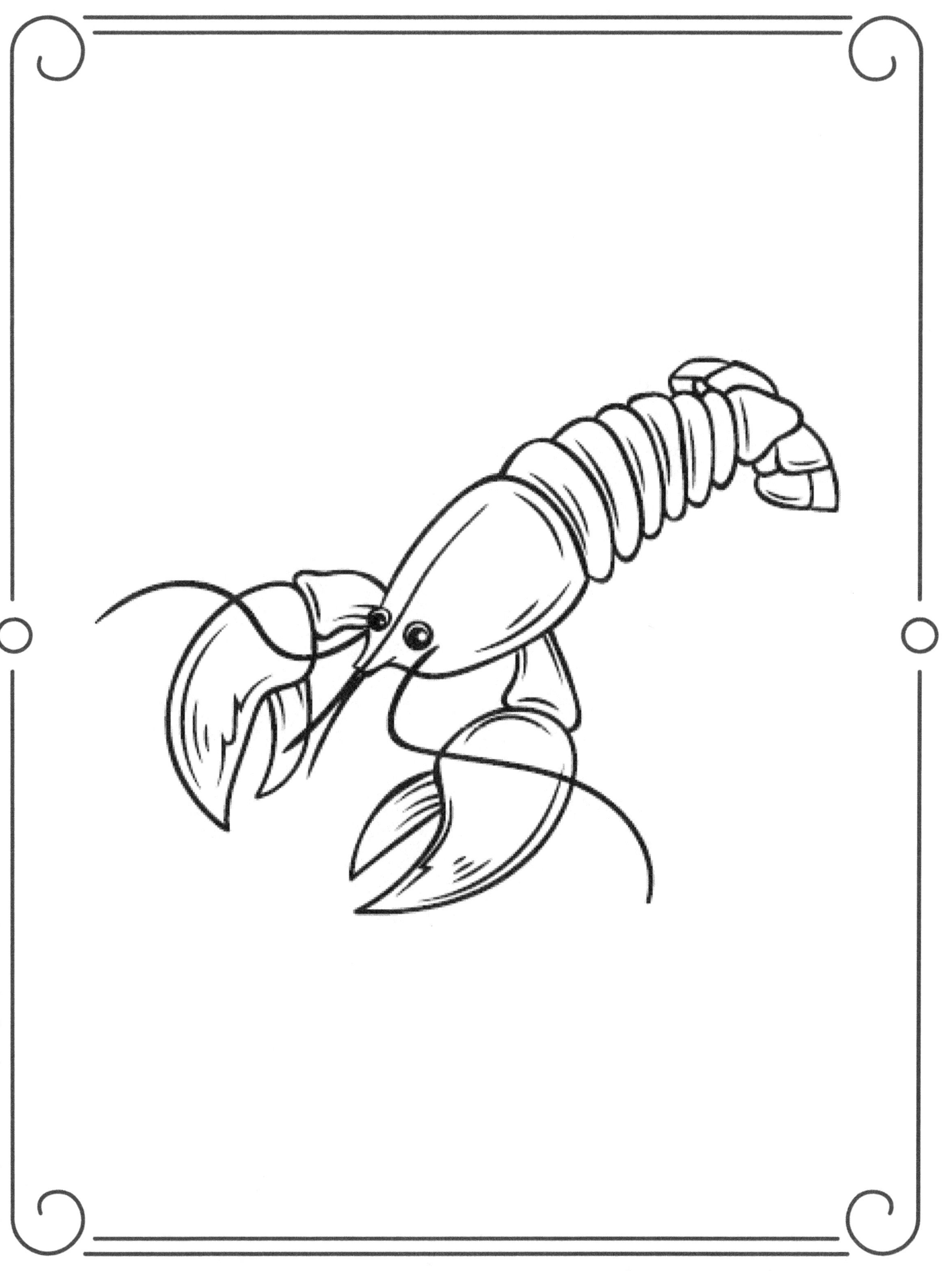

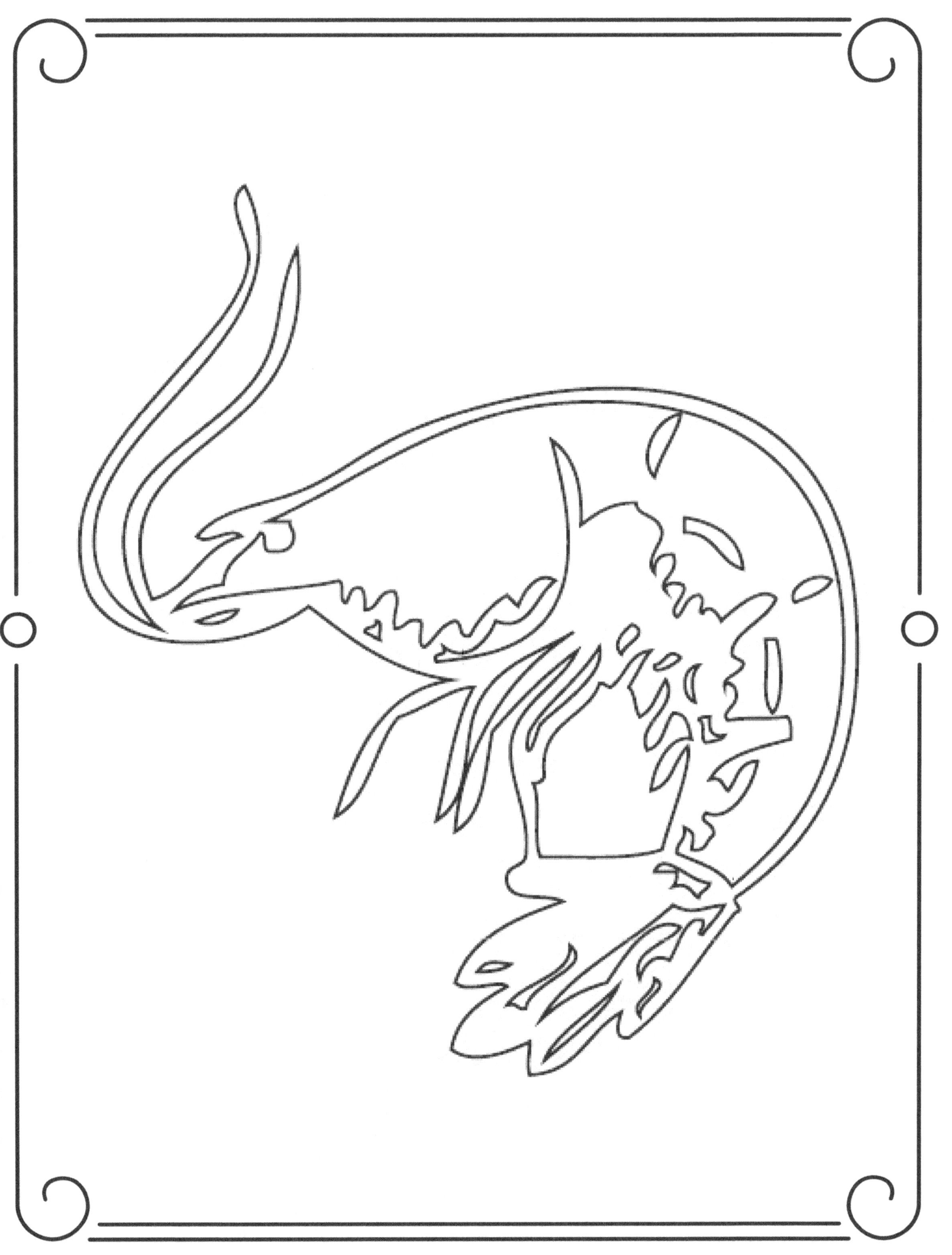

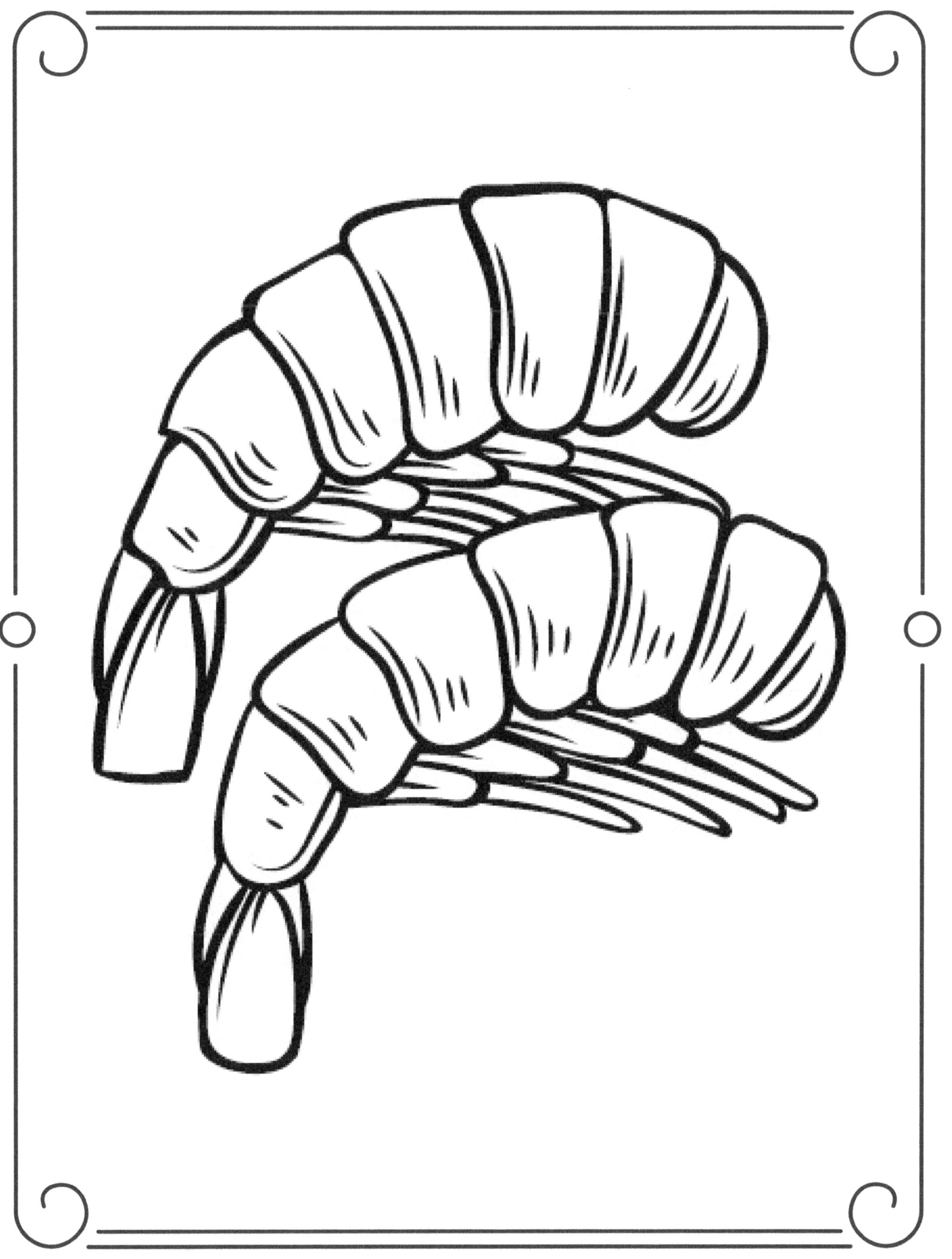

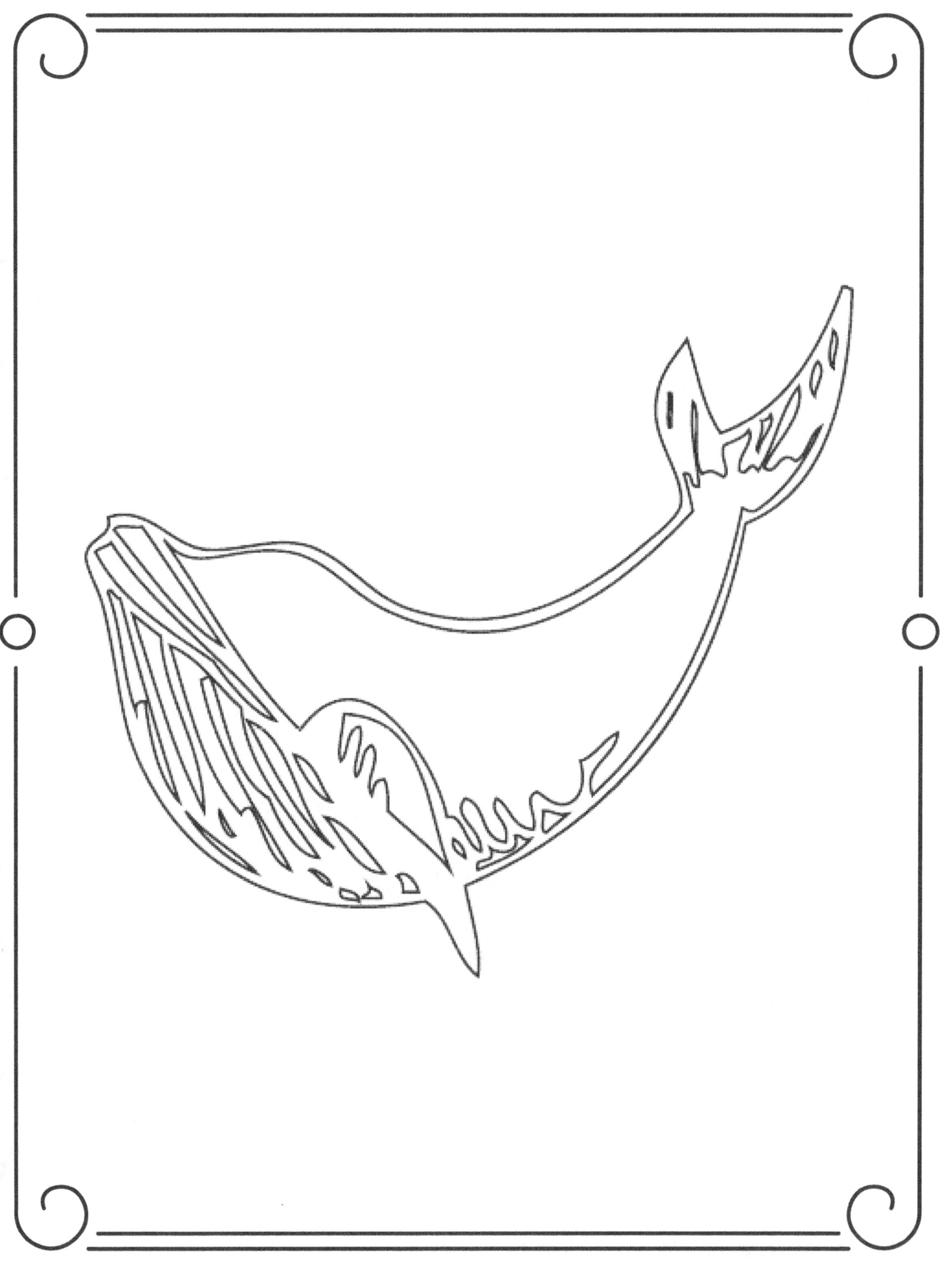

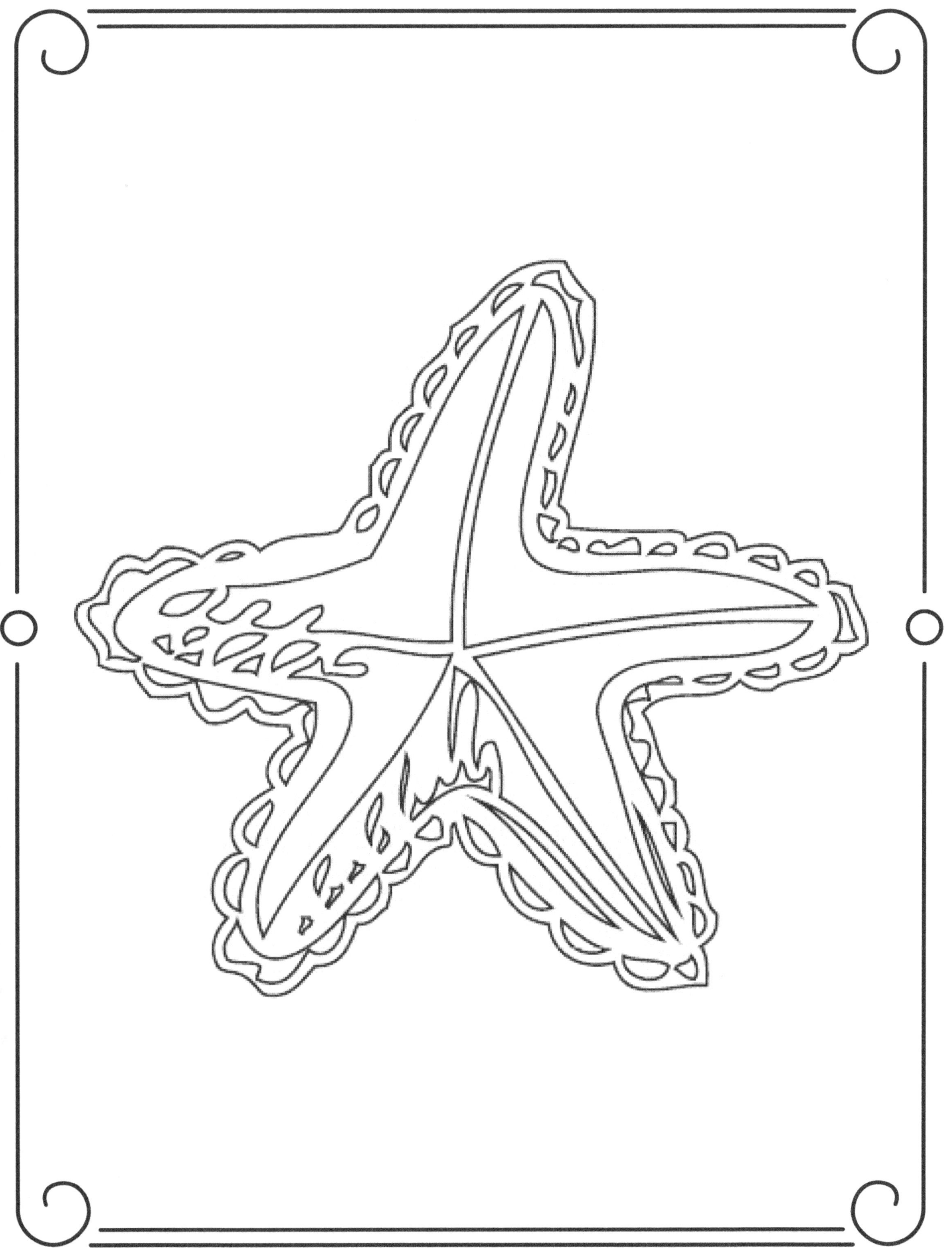

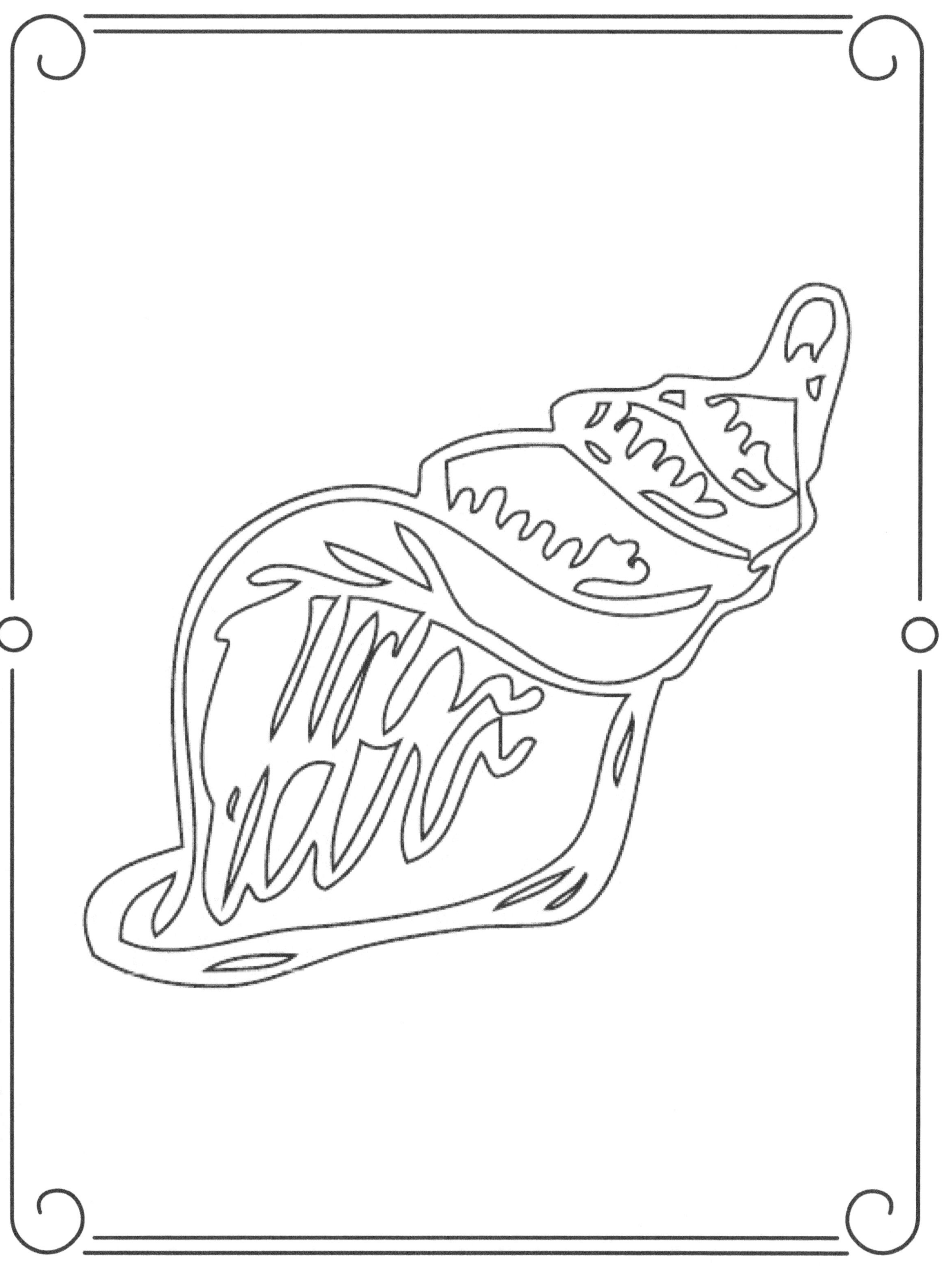

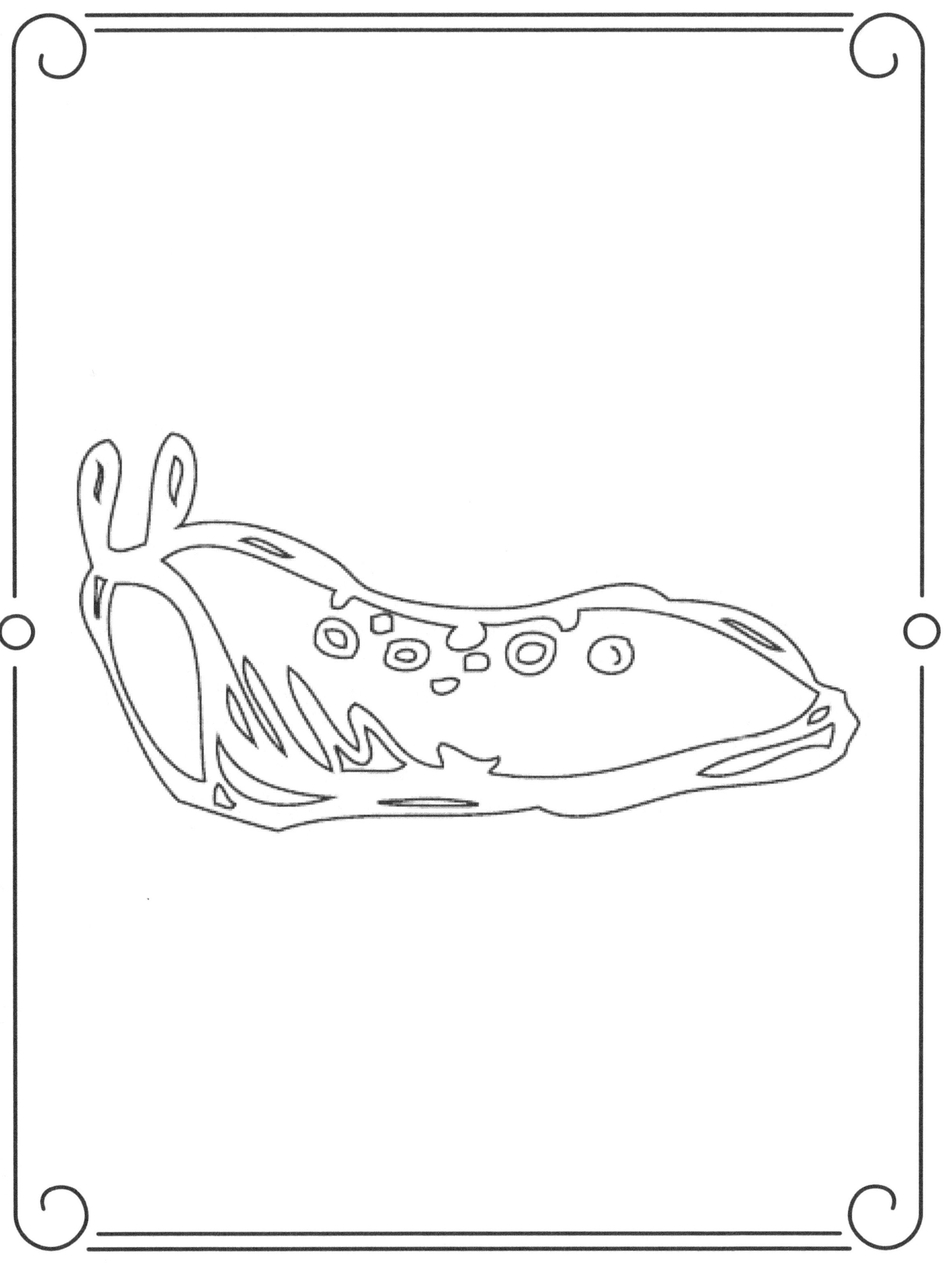

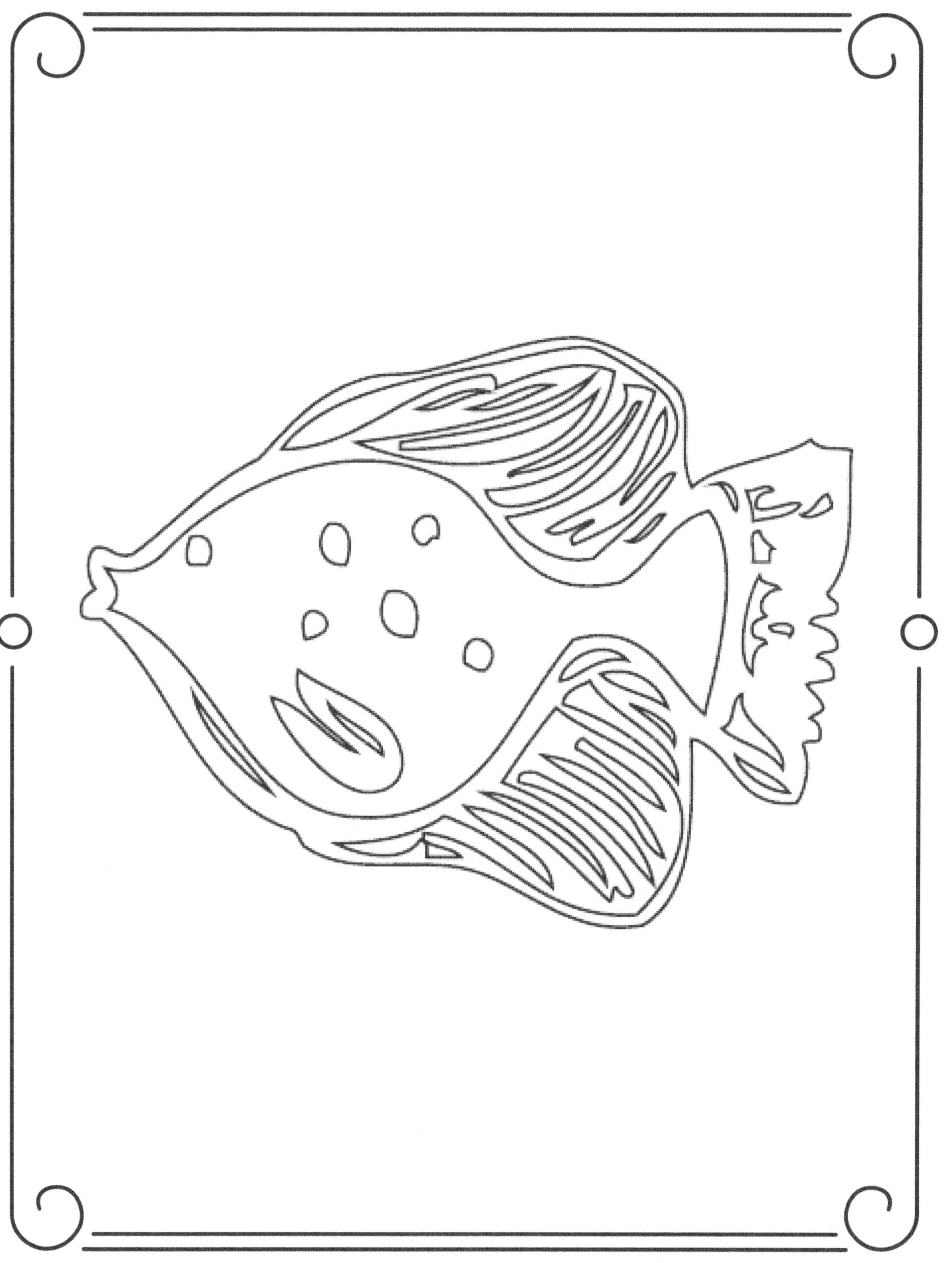

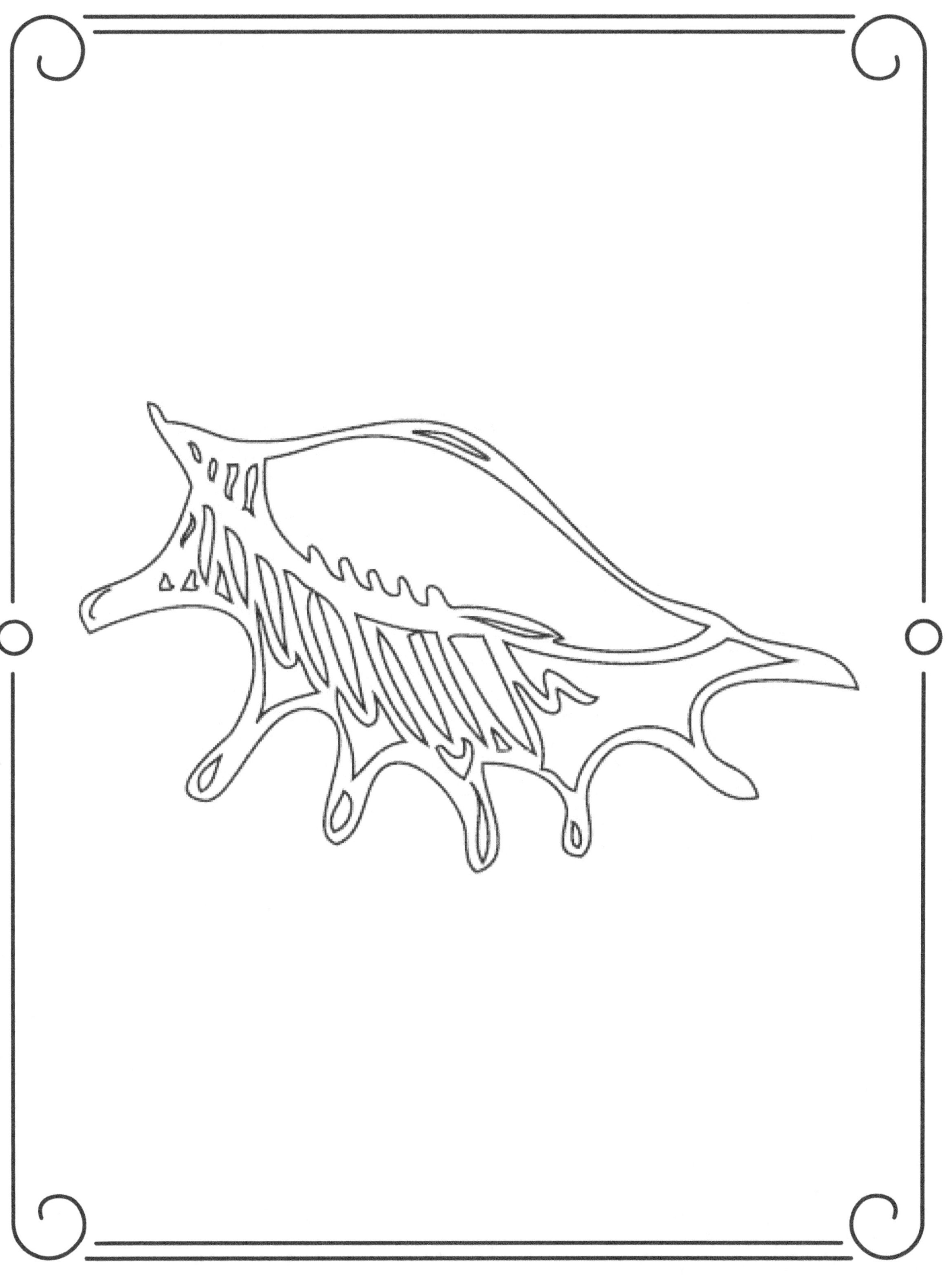

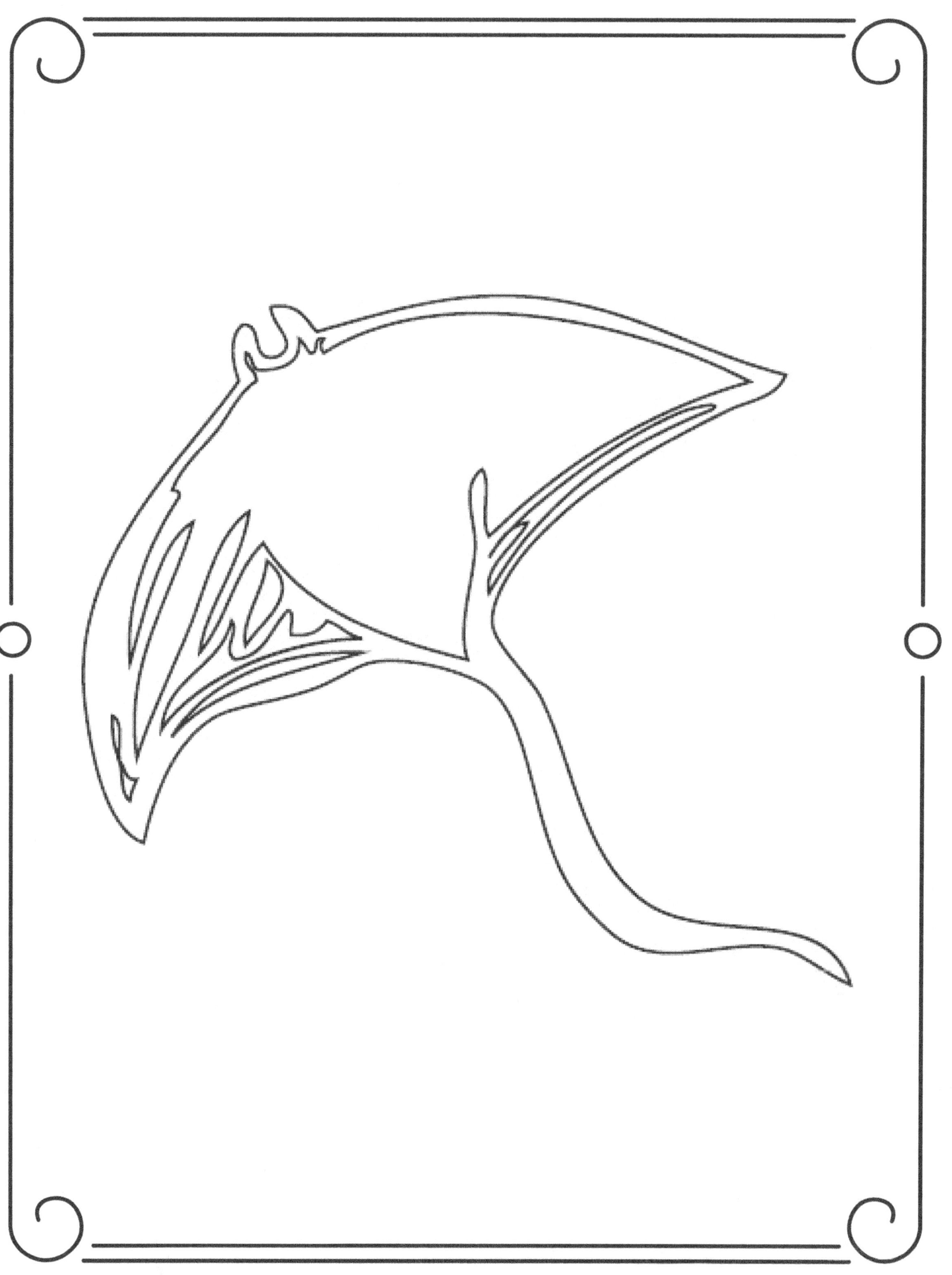

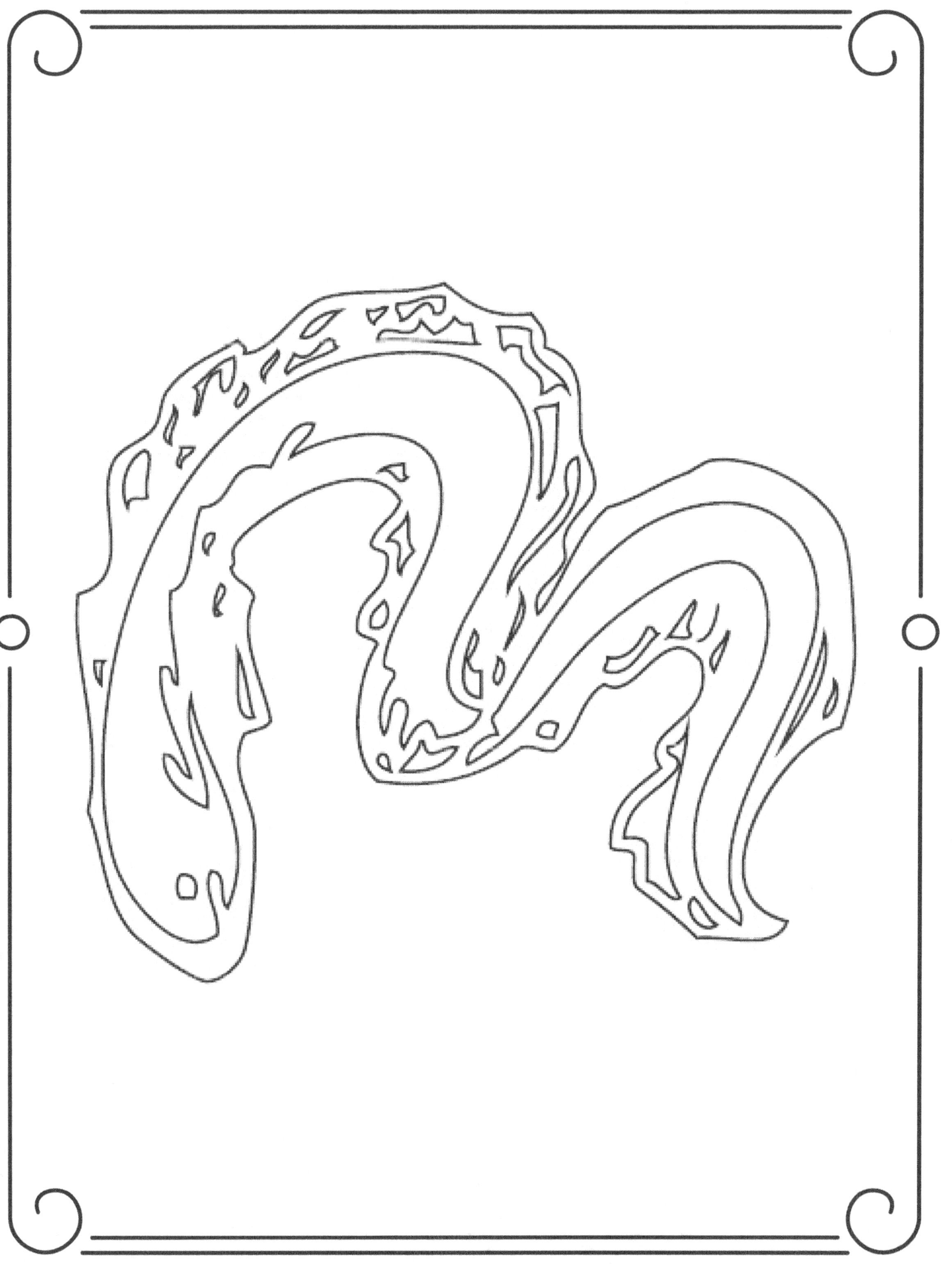

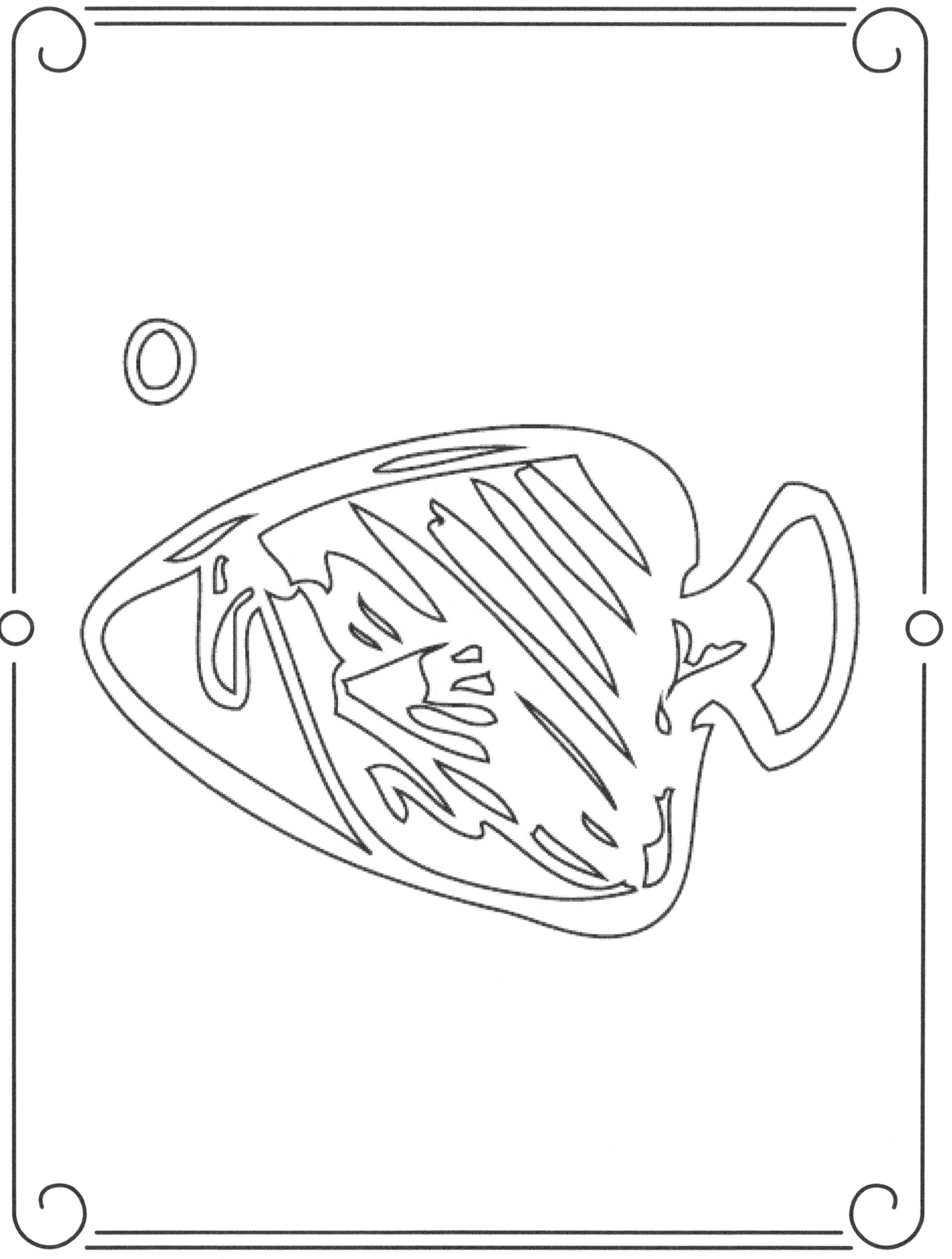

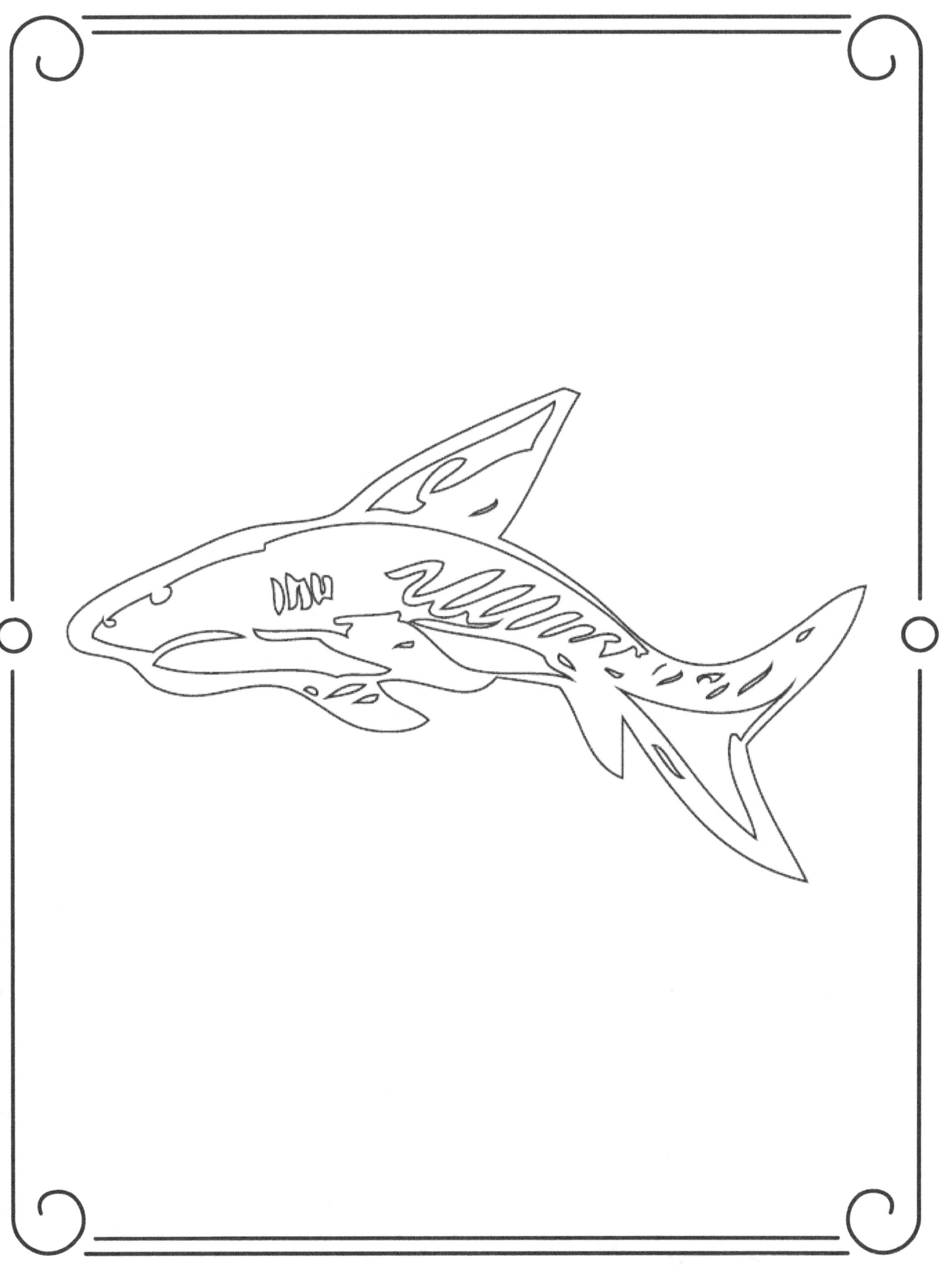

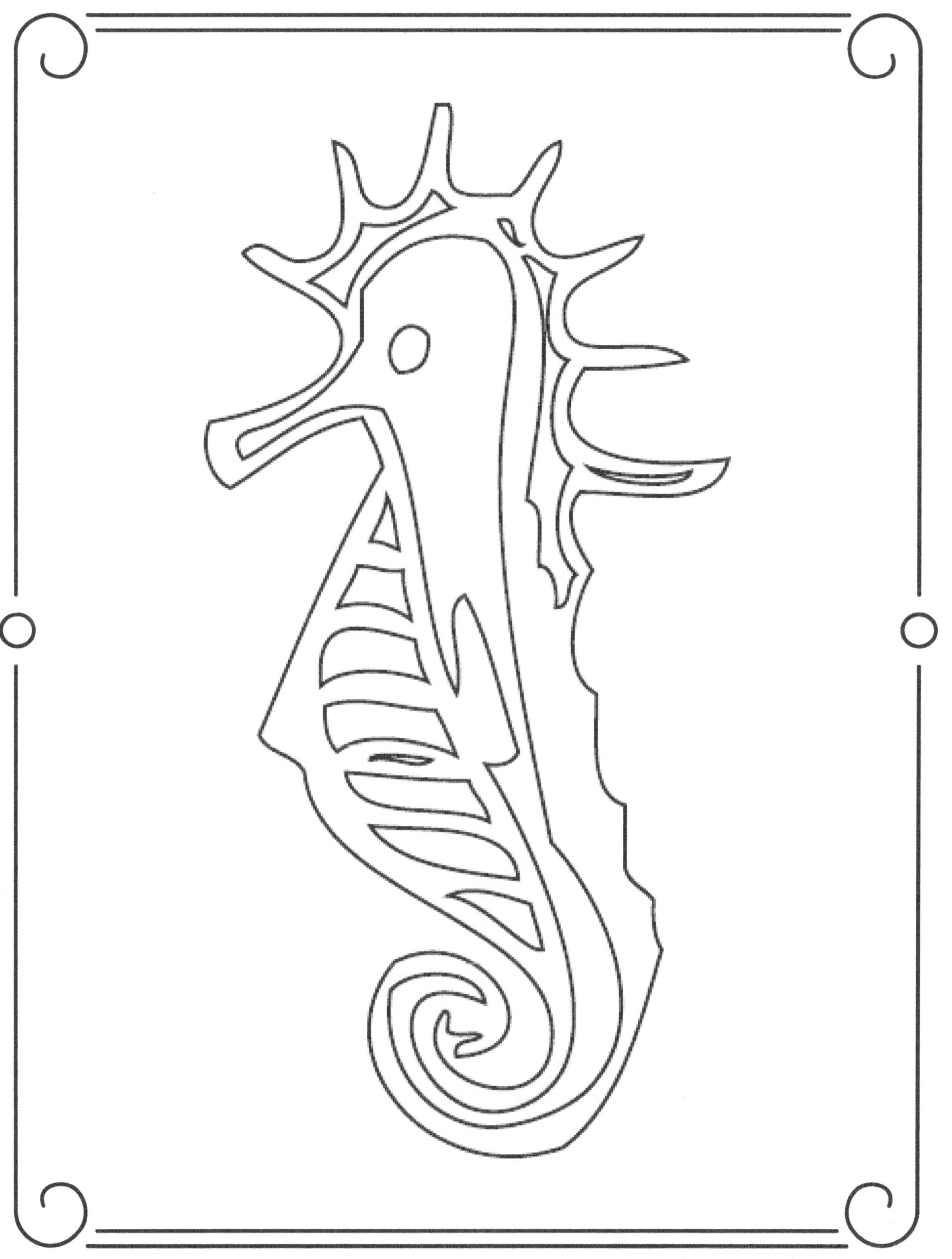

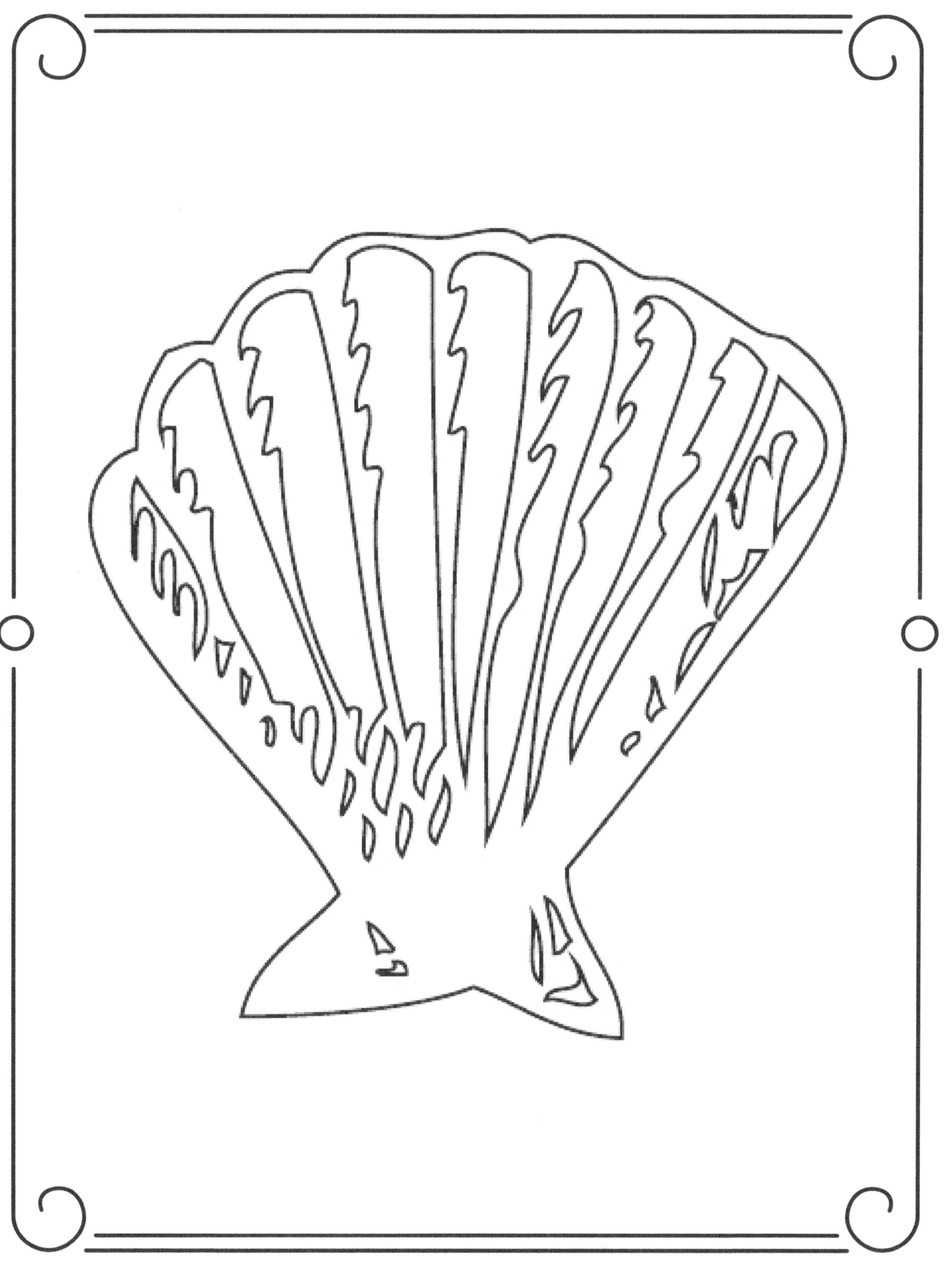

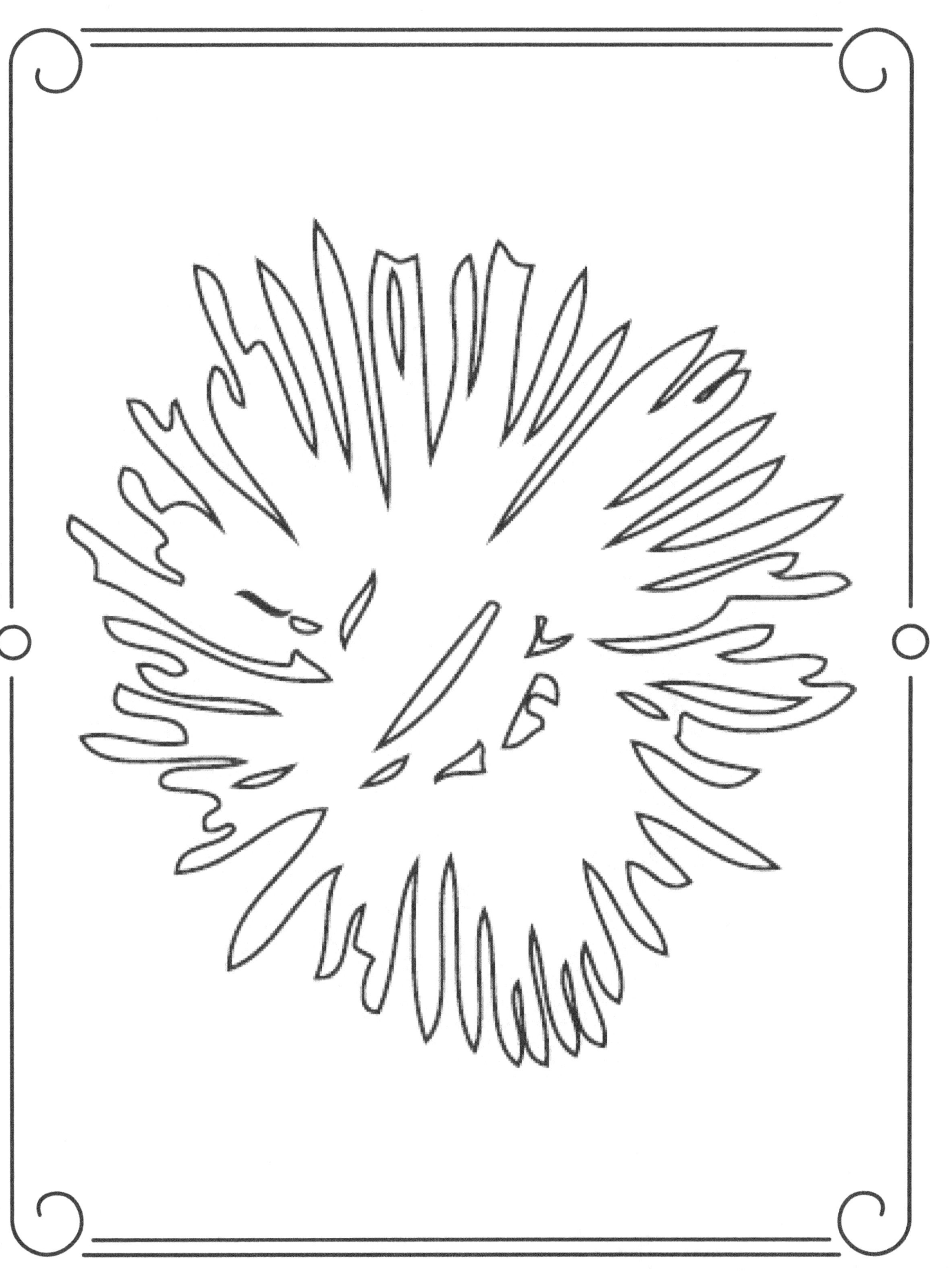

www.ingramcontent.com/pod-product-compliance
Lightning Source LLC
Chambersburg PA
CBHW080225260726
48658CB00008B/3004